AF412586

Discussion guide

IF YOU
PROMISE
NOT TO
TELL

by joe wayman

ISBN 0-945799-05-5

INTRODUCTION

This booklet is intended as a discussion guide for parents, teachers and anyone working with children. The purpose of this book is to help children explore and come to terms with their own feelings and to experience a more positive sense of self. The goal of these discussions is to help children realize they are not alone in their feelings; that we all experience the same hope, fear, pain and joy.

There is no beginning or sequence to the use of the poems or the discussion questions. You may use them as you choose and in response to the interest of your children. Make these explorations fun, relaxed and enjoyable. Allow as much freedom of expression as you can and respect the child's opinion. There are no "right" or "wrong" answers to these questions. They are simply designed to stimulate thinking about one's self and one's feelings.

1

For those of you in the classroom I would encourage the use of several kinds of grouping. Use them at different times and in different combinations:

> Get your students into partners and let them discuss a specific question all at the same time. You may wish to switch partners and discuss the same question again, or discuss several questions before changing partners.

> Get your students into groups of three to five and encourage them to discuss specific questions. Let the entire class do this at the same time. You can then move to large group discussions.

> Large group discussions seem to work best when one of the above formats is used first. The first two groupings are of a much lower risk level than sharing ideas in front of the entire class.

One last note. These discussion questions are also excellent for writing in a personal journal. Anything written in a personal journal should be considered private. Students should not be expected to share anything in their journal unless they so choose.

I hope these questions will serve as a springboard into a deeper understanding of feelings and lead to a greater sense of positive self-esteem.

PARENT PERSPECTIVE

This guide may be used effectively and affectionately by you, Mom and Dad, to help your children grow and learn about themselves and others. While much of this guide has suggestions for teachers who are working with larger groups of children, each and every discussion question may be used by you with your own children.

A few suggestions may help you initiate discussions with your child:

Don't insist on responses from your child on every question.

Be willing to share your point of view as well as asking for your child's.

Respond informally when your child is reading the poems and seems interested in talking about them.

Don't expect your child and you to agree on all responses. Respect your child's opinion.

SOMETIMES READ POEMS ALOUD to your child. And when your child wishes, let them read aloud to you.

Try not to put on your "teacher" hat with these ideas. Rather, participate with your child. Have fun, relax and explore these ideas with your entire family.

CORNERS

Differences
Relationships

In what ways is your life like the life of your best friend?

How is your life different from someone your age living in:
   a.   The arctic?
   b.   Africa?
   c.   Asia?

How are your lives the same?

Think of a "corner" of your life that you would like to share and talk about it with a partner.

Describe what you think of as a small "corner" of your life.

See if you and a partner can find three corners of your lives which are similar and three which are different.

I HATE TO WAIT

Patience
Promptness

Complete the following statement: I most hate to wait for....

Why do people always seem to be in a hurry?

What do you do when you are waiting for someone or something to happen?

What is the difference between waiting for a friend to arrive and waiting for your birthday?

Are you ever in a hurry to grow up?

What is meant by "all good things come to those who wait"?

What do you think is meant by "patience is a virtue"?

Describe a time when you had patience and a time when you ran out of patience.

ROGER'S DAD
DOING TIME

Relationships
Friends

When you have a disagreement with someone, do you:
  a. Avoid that person for a long time?
  b. Try to work it out somehow?
  c. Try to make the other person change?

Why do you think we all sometimes fight?

Why do we all sometimes seem to brag or boast?

Is it important to you to have a "big" mom or dad?

Describe a time when you were envious or jealous of a friend.

What do you think is the difference between reporting something and tattling?

When do you seek an adult's help to solve a problem and when do you try to solve it yourself?

Why is it important to have rules and people to enforce them?

Do you think we have too many or too few rules?

ALL DRESSED UP

Self Concept
Independence
Confidence

What do adults do that make you feel good about yourself?

What do your friends do that make you feel good or bad about yourself?

Describe your favorite outfit to a friend and why you like to wear it.

Bring a favorite shirt or blouse to school, share in small groups why it is your favorite.

Share an item of clothing that has sentimental value for you.

I feel best when:
    a. I am all dressed up.
    b. In my pajamas.
    c. I can get dirty and not worry about it.

Wear an outrageous color combination to school. Talk about people's reactions with a partner.

What do you think "dress for success" means?

BABY SISTER'S BLANKET

Trust
Security

On what things do you tend to depend? A teddy bear? A blanket? A friend? Sibling? Parent? Other?

Discuss "security blanket". What does it mean? What makes you feel secure?

Are security and safety the same thing?

What things do people depend on at different ages in their lives?

Do you have a lucky charm? Why does it make you feel secure?

Do you have any superstitions? What are they?

Discuss the idea that rituals or ceremonies make people feel secure.

Why do you think the unknown feels so risky?

SISTERS, SISTERS

Relationships
Siblings
Friends

Do you feel that you are always correct? Share a time your brother, sister or other family member was right and you were wrong.

A wise woman once said about disagreements: "Being right is not important, but understanding is." What do you think she meant?

Do you think boys and girls are more alike or more different in the way they solve disagreements?

Do you get along better with boys or girls? Why do you think that is true?

If you are an only child, what advantages or disadvantages do you think you have?

What would it be like to have 10 brothers and sisters?

Do you think boys or girls get into trouble more often? Why?

MOTHER, DO I HAVE TO?

Independence
Freedom
Choices

If you have a sibling, what kinds of things do you choose to do together? Separately?

How independent should someone your age be?

How would you feel if someone you admired didn't want you around?

Do you think you should have to do certain things? When do you think you need discipline?

At what age should you become independent? Will you ever be completely independent?

How does a person learn to be responsible? For what things are you responsible in your family?

In what ways are you responsible for your brother? Sister? Pet? Friend? Family? Parents?

RICKAFRITZ AND RACKAFRATZ

Anger
Frustration

When you get angry at a family member, what do you usually do? Does that behavior usually help? What might you do that would be more helpful?

Some people curse when they get angry. Others curse because they think it is cool. Do you think cursing makes you more grown up or cool?

What frequently goes wrong for you? What do you do about it?

Write a short story with the beginning:
I thought it would be a good day, but...

What frustrates you most at home? School? Play?

What do you do that is frustrating for another family member?

What do you do to let go of anger and frustration?

How does laughter help ease frustration? Do you ever laugh at yourself?

RUNNING

Winning
Differences

What does "letting off steam" mean to you? What do you do to let off steam?

Why do you think children like to run?

Why do adults keep telling kids not to run?

What things do you do for fun that grown-ups seldom do?

Why is running across a field so much fun?

Describe what would happen if people could run 70 mph?

Describe a time when you won a race with another person. Also describe a time you lost. How did you feel each time?

What is meant by "slow and steady wins the race"?

If running is so much fun, what would you do if you could never run again?

BELLY BUTTON BLUES

Self Concept
Independence
Confidence

What physical attribute do you have of which you are proud?

What attribute do you have of which you are not so proud?

How important do you think it is to be beautiful? Can you be successful and happy and not be beautiful?

What does "beauty is in the eyes of the beholder" mean to you?

What makes you laugh?
What makes you cry?

List all the buttons you can think of.

Would you be a button, a snap or a zipper? Why?

How would you feel if you were a lost button?

What does it mean to have the "blues"? What is the opposite of having the "blues"?

If you could rename a belly button, what would you call it?

KITE

Independence
Freedom
Choices

Like the kite in the poem, what would you do if you were completely free to do anything you wanted?

Would you choose to be totally free with no responsibilities, or responsible for another person or pet?

In what ways do you think people are like kites?

If you could be a kite, what color, size and shape would you be?

What things in your life are like the string on a kite? How?

How is a kite string like "mother's apron strings"?

Which of the following is most important:
   a. Independence?
   b. Dependence?
   c. Inter-dependence?

Are you ever rambunctious? When?

What do you do to calm down?

ROCKING CHAIR

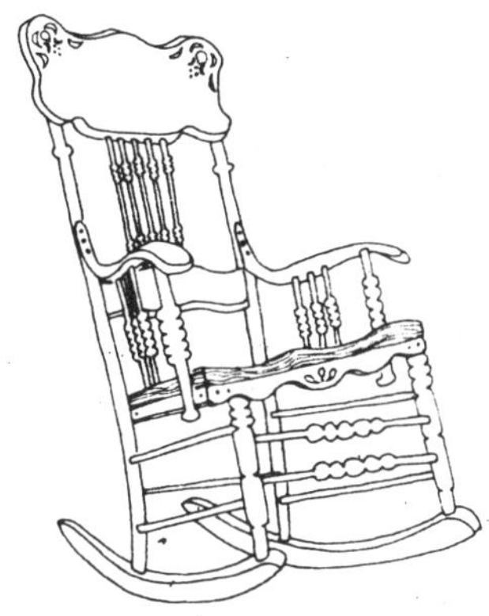

Trust
Security

How many people do you really trust?

Do you trust different people for different things or reasons?

When do you feel safe? What makes you feel unsafe? Is it important to always feel safe?

How important is your family in helping you feel safe and/or secure?

Share your ideas about feeling safe and taking risks.

What makes you feel safe besides your family?

Discuss the phrase "whistling in the dark".

Why do you think a rocking chair is a symbol of trust and security?

What are some other symbols of trust and security?

WATERMELON SUMMER

Myths
Choices
Seasons

What other foods do you associate with summer? With other seasons?

What are some things you like about a picnic? What do you not like?

Working with a partner, list everything you can think of for a successful picnic.

What are some of your favorite things to do in the summer? Winter? Spring? Fall?

Swallowing a watermelon seed causes a vine to grow from your nose is a myth used in the poem. What is a myth? What other myths do we have that we tell but don't really believe?

Watermelon is a fun food. What other foods do you consider fun?

If you were to rename this poem, what would you name it?

Try writing another poem about a different kind of summer.
(Popsicle Summer, Sidewalk Summer or Barefoot Summer)

WHERE IS A RAINBOW?

Imagination
Emotions

What is meant by "seeing rainbows in your heart"?

Have you ever been told something by an adult that you wanted to challenge?

Do adults always have the right answers?

For you, is a rainbow more of a scientific phenomenon or more of an emotional experience?

If you could find your "pot of gold" at the end of a rainbow, what would it be?

What do you think is meant by someone "always chasing rainbows"?

If you could touch a rainbow, how would it feel?

If a rainbow could talk, what would it say?

Write a conversation between yourself and a rainbow.

FLOWERS

Symbols
Caring

When you send someone flowers, what messages are you sending?

Flowers are a symbol. What other symbols can you think of and what messages do they send? (Eagle, flag, fig leaf, oak tree)

Describe a time you gave a present to a friend for no reason.

Do you think we ever give gifts out of obligation?

What could you do for an ill person besides send flowers?

If you were ill would you rather receive:
   a.   Flowers?
   b.   A visit from a friend?
   c.   A long letter from someone far away?

How would you feel if you received flowers but didn't know who sent them?

Which would you be if you had the choice and why:
   a.   Geranium?
   b.   Dandelion?
   c.   Tulip?

A ROSE IS A ROSE
NOT A WITCH, NOT A WITCH

Letting go
Caring
Misunderstanding

Share a time when you thought you didn't like someone but later you became friends.

Do you think most older people like children? Put up with them? Enjoy having them for short visits?

Ask an adult in your family to go with you to visit an older person who perhaps lives alone. After your visit write down three feelings you had and share them in class.

How do you think kids misunderstand elderly people? How do you think elderly people sometimes misunderstand kids?

How do you think people sometimes insulate themselves against pain? Sadness? Loneliness?

What do you think is meant by "wall of lace"?

How do you show kindness to elderly people?

How do they show kindness to you?

Did you ever have a friend who seemed to smother you with friendship? How did you handle it?

Discuss why the rose died when the snow was taken away. What did it mean to be insulated against the cold?

MY SPECIAL SECRET

Trust
Security

What one thing is most important in a friendship?

Do you think you are trustworthy? Dependable?

Have you ever heard a secret you shouldn't have? Did you keep it?

On a scale from 1 to 10, rate your own trustworthiness.

Under what conditions should you break a confidence?

What kinds of things do you think a person should keep secret? What about politicians? Clergy? Physicians?

Write something about one or more of the following:
  a. Living with a secret is like...
  b. When you would tell a secret for someone's own good.

Describe a time you told someone a secret, then found out they had told someone else. How did you feel? What did you do?

ME, MYSELF AND I

Self Concept
Confidence
Independence

What things give you confidence and what things make you feel inept?

Does how you feel about yourself depend upon what others think?

What do you do now that you think you will do better when you are older?

What do you like to do by yourself? How often do you do things by yourself?

What might it mean to "miss yourself"?

What does it mean in the poem to be a social creature? How are you social? How are you unsocial?

Do you ever have conversations with yourself?

If you were to write yourself a letter, what would you tell yourself?

<u>BILLY WAYNE ROGER ALPHONSO THE THIRD'S FAVORITE</u>

Relationships
Siblings
Friends

Talk to a friend and find out three things that you like that your friend doesn't like.

Why do you think people like different things?

Create a new ice cream flavor that might be your personal favorite.

Why do you think some peopole like simple things and others like more complex things?

How easily are you swayed from your opinion?

Do your friends ever make you change your mind?

How are our choices influenced by other people?

Name a favorite something of yours. Why is it your favorite?

What is the difference between moderation and going overboard? When do you tend to go overboard?

When might it be good to choose something other than you favorite?

How would you feel if you had NO choices?

OODLES OF NOODLES

Exaggeration
Directions

How does the author use exaggeration in this poem? Describe a time you exaggerated.

Is an exaggeration the same as a lie?

Is there ever a time when exaggeration is good?

Why do you think people exaggerate about things?

When is it important to follow directions carefully?

When is it important to figure out your own way of doing something?

What are some other ways you can think of to get rid of the noodles in the poem?

Why do some people not follow directions even when they are available?

BORED

Independence
Freedom
Choices

When you are bored, what do you do to get "un-bored"?

See if you and a partner can determine a meaning and some importance for this statement: Sometimes I sit and think and sometimes I just sit.

Do you think your parents are too strict or too lenient when they discipline you?

Is routine always boring?

When is routine a good thing?

How open are you to new things? New foods? Different clothes? Hair styles? New friends?

How do you decide to do something or not? Do your friends have any influence over that decision?

Would you rather:
  a. Clean your room or cut the grass?
  b. Take out the trash or go to bed?
  c. Wash windows or tend the baby?

PRETEND

Independence
Confidence

How would you feel if you were a baseball bat? A jump rope? A kangaroo?

Do you think it is important to pretend? Why or why not?

What do you sometimes pretend. Describe to a partner a daydream you sometimes have.

How are pretending and daydreaming alike? Different?

Talk over the differences between fantasy, reality and dreams.

What dreams do you have for your future?

If you could be any song, what song would you be?

How do you think a crocodile in a swamp feels? A crocodile in a zoo? A crocodile being hunted?

DOGGY, DOGGY
WHEN A GOLDFISH DIES

Pets
Responsibility
Caring

Share with a neighbor what you think are the responsibilities that go along with having a pet.

Do you always enjoy taking care of your pet? Why? Why not?

How would you feel if you were your pet and you hadn't been fed? Been walked? Been bathed? What would happen if you were suddenly your pet and your pet were you?

Why do you think some people care more about animals than they do about people?

Do you think people of different ages care about different things? Why?

Describe a time you lost a pet. How did you feel? What happened?

What do you think the phrase "time heals everything" means?

List healthy things for your pet. Now list unhealthy things.

Finish the following:
   If I had a kangaroo....
   If a hippopotamus followed me home...
   If I could have any pet in the world...

IN THE HAMPER
KITTEN
GHOST BUS
____

Fear
Courage

What are you afraid of that you think is probably an irrational fear?

What is a phobia? List some phobias people sometimes have. How do
you think people get them?

Why do you think night is more fearful than the day? How many
reasons can you think of?

Share several reasons why you think people are afraid of rats, snakes,
spiders, etc.

When are some things not as they seem?

Describe a time you made an honest mistake. What happened? Did it
cause you trouble?

Why do you think some animals should not be kept as pets?

Do you think some animals are naturally "bad"?

THE BOX

Fear
Courage

Are you most afraid of the dark, bees or of being lost?

If you had to choose one, which would you be:
  a. Snake?
  b. Cockroach?
  c. Tarantula?

When you are afraid, what do you do?

Discuss the meaning of "safety in numbers".

Do you think courageous people are ever afraid?

Do you think there are different kinds of fear? Explain what you mean?

Do your friends ever call you chicken? Describe a time, and explain what you did? How would you change your behavior if you could?

Some people panic and some people stay calm when they are afraid. Why do you think this happens?

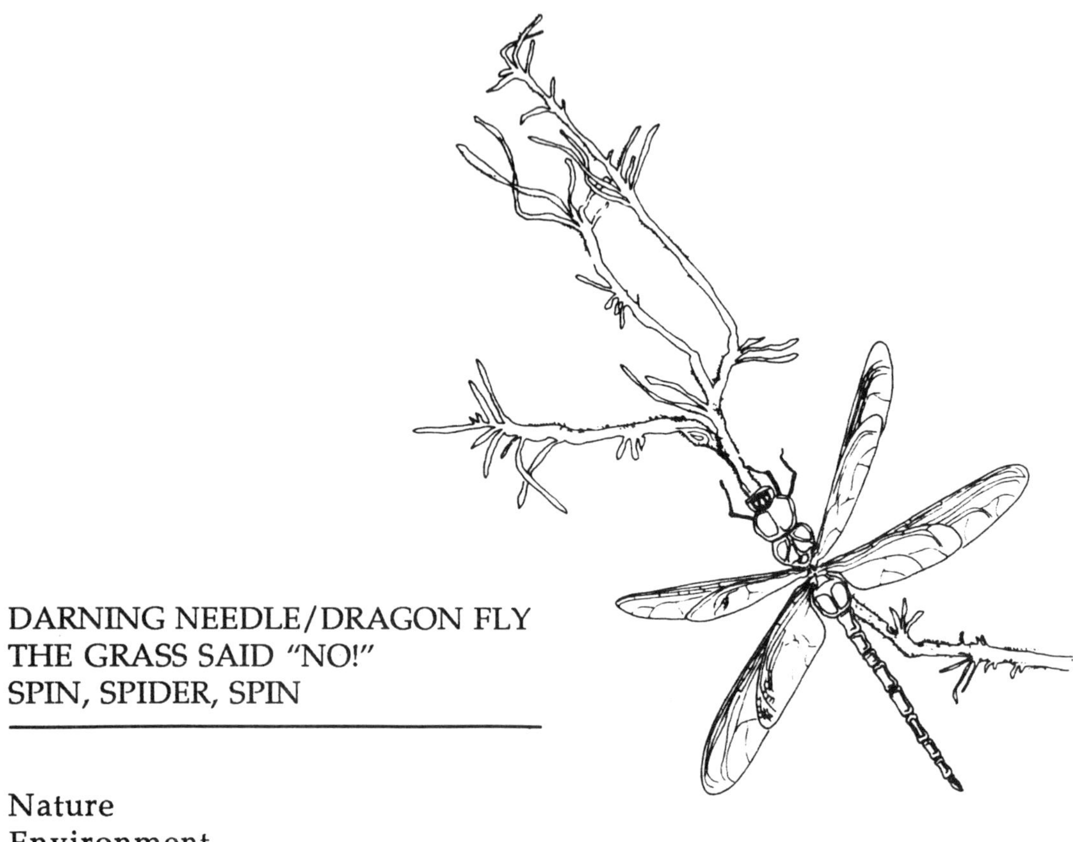

DARNING NEEDLE/DRAGON FLY
THE GRASS SAID "NO!"
SPIN, SPIDER, SPIN

Nature
Environment
Animals

What do you think our relationship to other creatures on this planet ought to be?

Do you think humans:
   a.   Own the earth?
   b.   Share the earth?
   c.   Govern the earth?

Do you think we should conquer nature or should we try to be a part of nature?

Why do you think the grass, the rain and the wind might say "NO!"?

What would a polluted river say if it could talk?

What would happen if the wind stopped blowing?

What might the wind say to an industrial smoke stack?

In what ways do we show respect for our environment? In what ways
do we abuse it?

Should we save our environment at all costs?

If you had to choose, would you be:
   a. A redwood tree?
   b. A water buffalo?
   c. An ocean?

Are animals important to you? Which ones? Why or why not?

Which would you be, a butterfly or a bee? A spider or a dragonfly? A
fish or a stream?

MOONLIGHT NIGHT

Favorite things

What is your favorite time of day?

What is the difference between dusk and twilight?

Do you like evening or morning better? Why?

In what ways can the darkest night be described as:
    a. Mysterious
    b. Lazy
    c. Exciting
    d. Pale

FLUTTER-BY/BUTTERFLY

Nature
Environment

Share a time when you killed a "critter" for no reason. How did you feel? Would you change your behavior?

Does a dead animal have the same beauty as a living animal?

Of what value is it to us to have zoos? Do you think we should or should not keep animals in zoos?

What do you think is the most beautiful and why:
   a. Ghost tiger
   b. Bat
   c. Butterfly

When is it necessary to kill certain animals?

Is using cows and chickens for food the same as hunting elephants for their tusks?

What do you think is the most beautiful animal on earth?

What do you think butterflies, seals and leopards have in common with each other?

QUESTIONS WITHOUT ANSWERS

Paradox
Life

Discuss the meaning of a paradox.

Discuss how a question is sometimes more important than the answer.

In what situations can there be more than one right answer?

When do we find out the important answers in life?

What does the needle in the haystack mean in this poem?

Choose one of the following and discuss it with a partner:
    a.   What good is age without the wisdom?
    b.   What good is time without the season?
    c.   What good is a window without glass?

What things in your life are like a race without an ending?

If you could have the answer to one question, what would it be?